Penguins on Parade

Lisa Marie Kelly

Antarctica

Antarctica is the fifth largest continent, bigger than Europe. Nearly all of Antarctica is buried under snow and ice. Penguins like to live where it is cold.

Blizzard

Winds from the South Pole blow air that is thick with snow to form blizzards. The penguins stand shoulder to shoulder to make a wall against the snow until the storm is over.

Creche

Chicks join together in unattended groups called creches. These are for protection and warmth while both parents get food.

Dive

Penguins dive underwater to catch food. They can dive up to 900 feet.

Eggs

Eggs are laid once each year by
the female. Eggs can be white,
blue, or green.

Flippers

A penguin's wings are like flippers for swimming and for balance. They cannot fly.

Guard

The first 3 weeks of a chick's life is known as the guarding stage. Adults must constantly watch the chicks.

Harm

There are many things that harm penguins. Brown skuas and leopard seals eat penguins. People also hunt penguins for their feathers.

Incubation

Incubation is the time period that
is required for the eggs to hatch.
Eggs are held on the feet close
to the body for warmth.

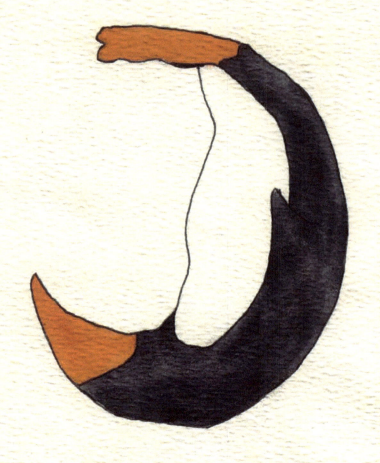

Jump

Some penguins jump around.

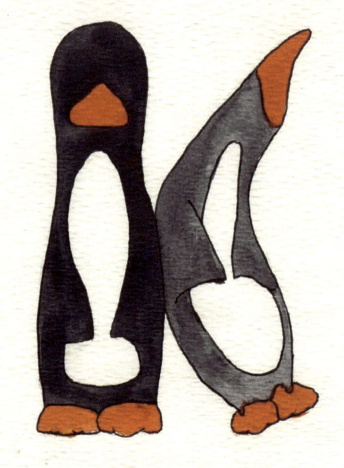

King

The king penguins are one
of the largest type of birds.

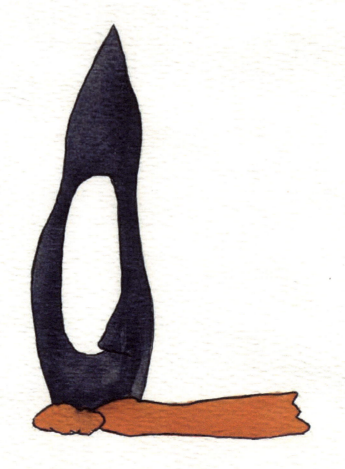

Landings

Penguins get on to land by shooting straight up out of the water and landing on their feet.

Molting

Molting is when penguins shed their old feathers and grow new ones. They must stay out of water during this time.

Nesting

Most penguins build nests
when they lay eggs. Nests
are usually built with stones.

Oily

The feathers of penguins
are oily to keep them warm
and waterproof.

Porpoising

Porpoising is when penguins dive in and out of the water like dolphins. This allows them to move fast and take in air.

Quick

Most penguins are quick in
the water and on land.

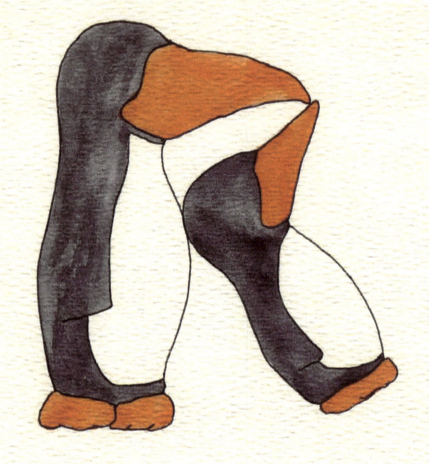

Rookery

A rookery is a colony of penguins. One million birds can live in a rookery.

Swim

Most penguins are strong,
fast swimmers and can swim
up to 15 mph.

Toboganing

Tobogganing is when penguins slide on their stomachs. This allows them to move fast.

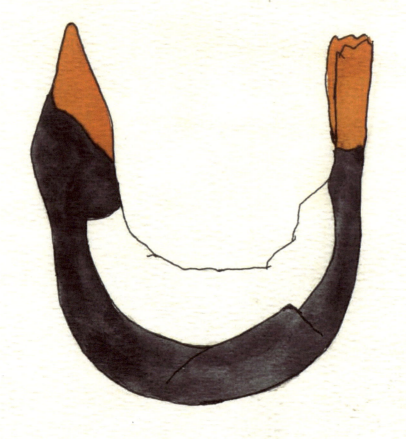

Underwater

Some penguins can stay underwater up to an hour.

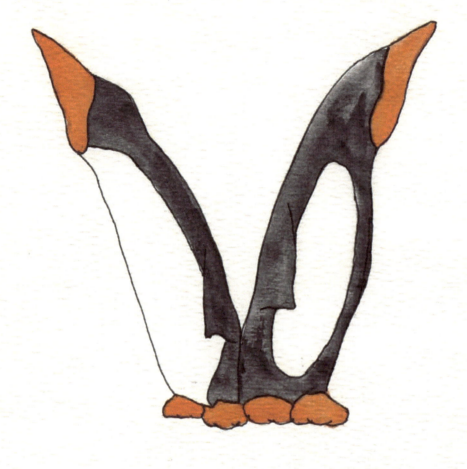

Variety

There are 18 different kinds of penguins. They vary in size and shape.

Waddle

On land, penguins walk by
waddling due to short legs.

Xylophone

I have never heard a penguin
play a xylophone.

Young

Young chicks feed on food
from their parent's mouth.

Zoo

Many penguins can
be seen at the zoo.

www.ingramcontent.com/pod-product-compliance
Lightning Source LLC
Chambersburg PA
CBHW041422050326
40689CB00002B/620